Fundamental

VOLLEYBALL

Thanks to Coach Lynne McDonald and the following members of the Mosquito Coast Volleyball Club:

Charleen Anderson,
Rebecca Bauer,
Heather Canonico,
Deanna Foss,
Jill Gowling,
Sarah Runka,
Christina Rybak,
Lisa Shanblott,

and coaches Bob Stanek and José Jones, and the following members of the Team 'Sota Volleyball Club:

Tim Dougherty,
Jonathon Drankwalter,
Brad Johnson,
Flynn McKeegan,
Danny Seppala,
Ryan Smith,
Adam Southwick,
and Kyle Westbrook,

who were photographed for this book.

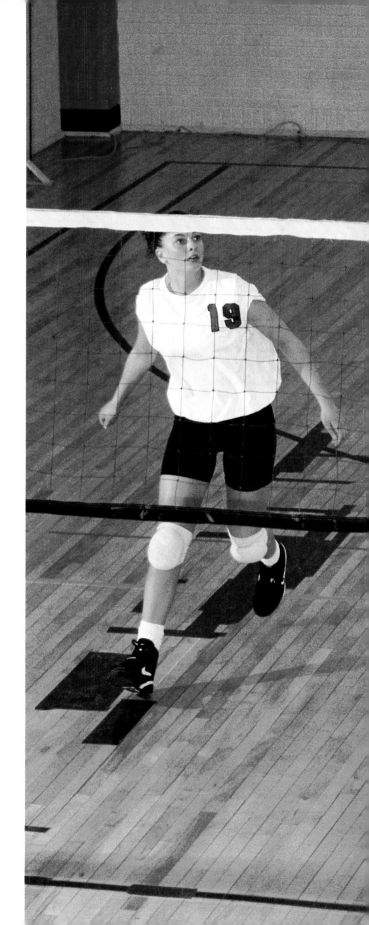

Contents

HOW THIS GAME GOT STARTED

Imagine being one of six players diving, lunging, and scrambling to keep the ball from hitting the floor on your side of the court. Then picture yourself smacking the ball down to the other side of the net for a game-winning point. With its thundering spikes, spectacular digs, and spirit of teamwork, volleyball is a sport full of fun and action.

Volleyball is a game of nonstop motion because the ball must be kept moving. Players don't catch and throw the ball to each other. Instead, they tap or pass it to teammates and hit it at opponents.

College volleyball is a fast-paced and exciting sport to watch. More than 1,000 colleges have volleyball teams.

7

The name, volleyball, indicates what William G. Morgan (pictured at left) had in mind back in 1895 when he introduced the sport at his Holyoke, Massachusetts, gymnasium. Morgan, who was the physical fitness director at the local Young Men's Christian Association (YMCA), wanted to combine some of the skills of baseball, handball, and tennis into a new sport. Morgan intended for the participants to volley the ball—bat it back and forth over the net—to develop teamwork while they got their exercise.

From that simple start, volleyball has grown into a sport that attracts thousands. Most high schools have volleyball teams for girls, and some offer the game for boys also. There are 1,200 colleges that field women's teams and 60 that have men's teams. Countless players enjoy their sport at YMCAs and recreation centers.

The United States Volleyball Association (USVBA) organizes teams and tournaments for players outside of the school competitions. In 1993, the USVBA had about 93,000 members. The USVBA also runs a large program for players ages 10–18, called the Junior Olympics Program. Some 48,000 young athletes participated in USVBA tournaments in 1993.

The USVBA also helps sponsor the U.S. Olympic teams. Every four years, at the Summer Olympic Games, the best volleyball teams in the world gather to compete for a gold medal.

One of the most exciting Olympics ever for American volleyball fans was in 1984, when the U.S. men's team won the gold medal and the women's team won the silver for second place. Then, in 1988, the American men again won the gold medal. Their winning streak was broken in 1992, however, when they finished second.

This book will introduce you to the basics of playing volleyball. Just as in any other sport, learning the skills and moves to play volleyball takes time and effort. But if you are patient and persistent, you can become a good volleyball player—maybe even an Olympian.

Gold in 1984

Although the game of volleyball was invented in the United States, athletes in other countries quickly adopted the sport. Players in Japan, China, Cuba, and the former Soviet Union were among those who became very skilled at volleyball. Teams from these countries were the best in the world.

The United States had never won an Olympic gold medal in volleyball, and the U.S. men's team in 1984 was determined to change that. The Americans began the Olympic Games on a 24-match winning streak, which included 4 victories over the tough Soviet team. None of the matches had been held in the United States.

The U.S. winning streak ended in the Americans' fourth match of the Olympics, when they were beaten by Brazil 15–12, 15–11, 15–2. But the defeat was in the pool-play, or round-robin, portion of the tournament. That meant that the U.S. team was not eliminated from the tournament. Five nights later, in the gold-medal final, the Americans defeated the Brazilian team 15–6, 15–6, 15–7, to win America's first gold medal in volleyball.

BASICS

Just like tennis and basketball, volley-ball is played on a court. The court is 29 feet, 6 inches wide and 59 feet long. It is divided by a net, which is usually more than 7 feet high. Sometimes the net is set at a lower height for beginners.

A line, called the **center line,** directly under the net divides the court. There are also lines on each side of the court, parallel to the net and about 10 feet away from it. These lines are called the **10-foot lines,** or **attack lines.**

The Ball

A volleyball is about the size of a soccer ball, but it is softer and lighter. It weighs about 9 ounces and has a circumference (distance around) of about 26 inches.

11

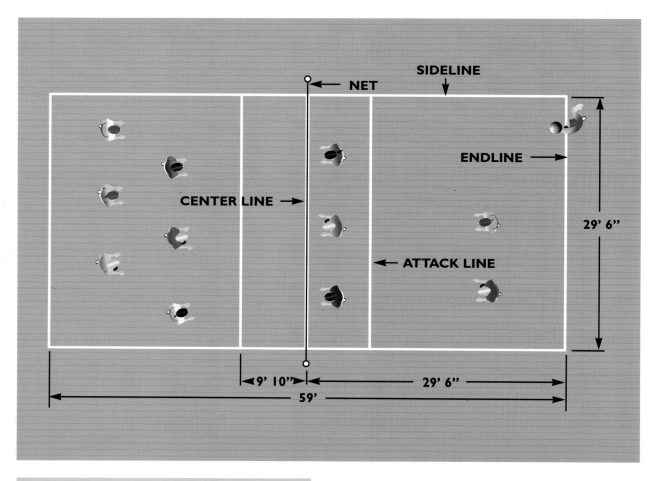

SIDELINE

NET →

← ENDLINE

CENTER LINE →

29' 6"

← ATTACK LINE

◄9' 10"►

29' 6"

59'

Faults

Volleyball rules are designed to keep the game fair and to keep the ball moving. Some violations of the rules are:

- *touching the net at any time*
- *stepping on or over the end line while serving*
- *stepping over the center line*
- *catching or throwing the ball*
- *hitting the ball more than three times on a side*
- *blocking when you are in a back row position*
- *spiking when you are in a back row position*
- *serving when it isn't your turn*

Rules

A volleyball team has six players. Sometimes, when people are practicing or playing just for fun, there are more people or fewer people on a team. When two teams are playing a real game, however, six is the correct number.

The object of the game is to hit the ball over the net so that it lands in the opponent's playing area. A team may hit the ball one, two, or three times to get it over the net. One player cannot hit the ball twice in a row, though. A team tries to prevent the ball from hitting the floor in its area.

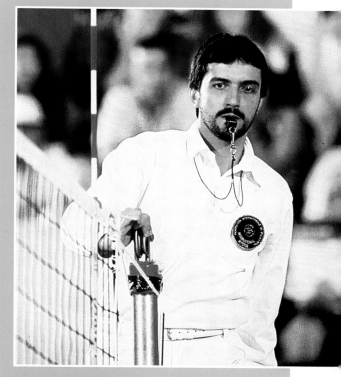

Only the serving team can score points in a volleyball game. So if the ball hits the floor on the receiving team's side, play stops and the serving team scores one point. The player in the right back position moves behind the end line to serve again.

If the ball hits the floor on the serving team's court, play stops and the receiving team gets to serve. The players on that team then **rotate,** or move clockwise one position, and the player who is now in the right back position serves.

If a hitter on the serving team hits the ball out of bounds, the receiving team gets to serve. But if a player on the receiving team touches the ball before it goes out of bounds, the serving team earns a point.

A game is played until one team scores 15 points. The winning team must have at least two more points than its opponent. If the score is 15 to 14, the game will continue until one team has two more points than the other. A series of games makes up a **match.** To win a match, a team must win two of three games or three of five games.

Players are either front row players, who play near the net, or back row players, who defend the back area of the court. Any player may pass or set the ball, but only players in the front row positions may spike or block it. These players usually play between the attack line and the net. No player can hit the ball two times in a row. That is a **fault.** Touching the ball while blocking does not count as one of a team's hits.

Calling the Game

When teams are playing a school or USVBA game, five officials will make sure all the rules of the game are followed. Sometimes, in recreational play, only one official is used.

The **first referee** is in charge of the match. He or she stands on a ladder at one end of the net so that he or she can watch all the action. The first referee signals for the players to serve and stops play when a player commits a fault.

The **second referee** stands on the floor at the other end of the net. She or he watches to make sure no players touch the net or step over the center line. This referee also supervises any substitutions the teams make.

A **scorekeeper** keeps track of the score, a team's substitutions, and timeouts at a table near the court.

The two **line judges,** at opposite corners of the court, signal if a ball is hit in the court or if it is outside the line.

To give you an idea of volleyball's basic maneuvers, we'll watch the practice sessions of two USVBA juniors teams—the Team 'Sota boys and the Mosquito Coast girls.

Serving

First, Charleen and her Mosquito Coast teammates are practicing their **serves**. Play starts with a serve, when one player hits the ball directly over the net into the other team's court. The ball cannot touch the net.

There are several ways to serve. The two most common serves are **underhand** and **overhand**.

Charleen is hitting an **underhand serve**. She holds the ball in one hand. Then, while stepping forward, she swings her other arm forward and hits the ball from below with her fist.

By changing her aim or the force with which she hits the ball, Charleen can keep her opponents guessing about where the ball will go. But she has to be sure that the ball stays inbounds, that is, within the court area.

If Charleen hits the ball too hard or off to the side, her serve will land outside the playing area. When her serve lands out of bounds, Charleen's team loses the serve and the other team gets to serve.

Clothing

T-shirts and shorts or sweatpants are what most people wear when playing volleyball. Don't wear anything that will get in your way or make it hard for you to move quickly. Wear gym shoes when you play so you can jump and run. Many players also wear knee pads to protect their knees when they lunge and dive for balls.

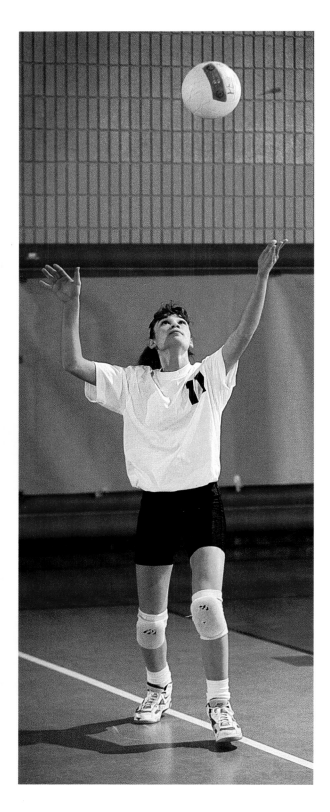

Another powerful serve is the **overhand serve,** which Charleen also likes to use. She starts this serve by tossing the ball up in the air slightly in front of her head. Charleen's other hand is pulled back behind her head, near her ear. As the ball comes down, Charleen swings her arm forward and hits the ball when it is just above her head. For power and control, Charleen hits the center of the ball with her open hand.

Think Positively

Some volleyball players imagine making a successful serve before they hit the ball. This is called visualization. To do this, imagine that you are serving. See yourself tossing up the ball, hitting it, and watching it go over the net and in. Some coaches and players believe that thinking about a serve helps a player to concentrate, and concentrating helps a player to serve correctly. You can do this for many sports activities, such as throwing a baseball, making a free throw in basketball, or serving in tennis. Just remember, open your eyes before you take your shot!

Passing

Next, the girls work on their **passing**. Players pass the ball to each other in order to set up a strong hit. To do the **forearm pass** (which is also called a bump pass), Jill locks her hands with her thumbs together. She keeps her arms extended away from her body until the ball hits them between her elbows and wrists. Notice that her knees are bent and that the ball hits her arms just above the wrists when the ball is about waist high.

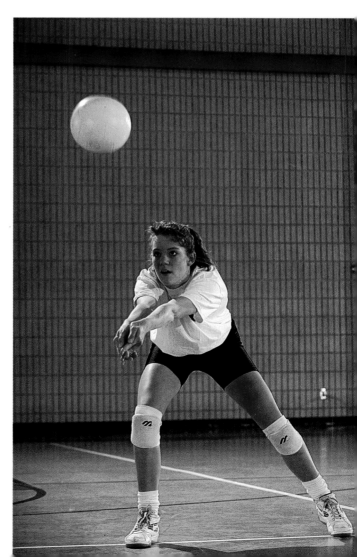

The Mosquitoes use a forearm pass if they are receiving a serve or if the other team has hit the ball with power. If the ball is gently hit over to their side of the court and they can contact it above their heads, the Mosquitoes use the **overhead pass**.

The Mosquitoes coach reminds Christina that it is important to watch the ball when using the overhead pass and to move quickly to get under it. Otherwise, Christina will be off balance when she touches the ball and she won't be able to control it.

Christina stands with her knees and elbows bent. Her arms are above her head and her fingers are spread wide open. She watches the ball through her fingers. Once the ball touches her hands, Christina guides the ball toward the ceiling and forward. Christina extends her fingers forward in a straight line after releasing the ball. **Following through** like that helps make sure the ball goes where Christina aims it.

Setting

A **set** is the link between the pass and the hit that sends the ball over the net. First a teammate passes the ball to the setter, who guides the ball to the hitter. The hitter then hits it over the net. Because the setter coordinates a team's movements, the setter is often called the "quarterback" of the volleyball team.

Danny is setting. He must anticipate

where the first pass will go and quickly move to that spot.

When Danny is the setter, he stands with his side to the net. He uses an overhead pass to try to place the ball about five feet higher than the net and about two feet from it. If the pass to Danny is below his waist, he uses a forearm pass to direct the ball to that same spot.

Spiking

The Team 'Sota players are always eager for this next drill. **Spiking** is the dramatic flourish of the game—volleyball's version of basketball's slam dunk. To spike, a hitter slams the ball over the net and down on the other side of the court.

Notice how Brad watches the ball as Danny sets it. When Brad sees Danny start to set the ball, Brad quickly takes several running steps—his **approach**—toward the net. Then he stops, brings both feet together, and jumps straight up. The running start gives Brad enough momentum to jump and hit the ball when it is higher than the net.

At the top of his jump, Brad strikes the ball when it is above his head and slightly in front of him. Hitting the ball with an open hand gives Brad a powerful shot. He brings his arm forward for his follow through, but is careful not to touch the net. Touching or running into the net is a fault, which means Brad's team would be penalized.

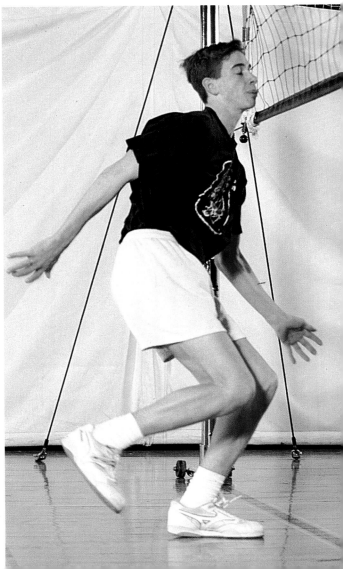

Flo Hyman's Spiking Legacy

One of the most famous spikers in American volleyball history was Flo Hyman. She was a 6-foot, 5-inch hitter on the U.S. Olympic team that finished second in the 1984 Olympics. That is the best the American women have ever done in the Olympics.

Flo said winning the silver medal was one of the proudest moments of her life. But it took her nine years of hard work on the U.S. team to achieve this goal.

Flo was a member of the first group of U.S. women who trained together just for the Olympics. They began working toward that goal in 1974. Before that, the U.S. team was an all-star team. Players from different teams all over the country came together just before they tried to qualify for the Olympics. Because they didn't know each other very well, they didn't play together as a team very well. As a result, the United States hadn't earned its way into the Olympics since volleyball had become an Olympic sport in 1964.

Flo and her teammates changed that in 1979 when they finished second in a qualifying tournament. This meant they were good enough for the 1980 Olympic Games. Despite the fact that Cuba took first, Flo was named the Most Valuable Player at the tournament.

But the long-awaited trip to the Games was not to be. President Jimmy Carter wanted to protest the former Soviet Union's war with Afghanistan. He ordered all American athletes to stay away from the Olympics because the Games were being held in Moscow.

Many athletes decided to give up their dreams of being in the Olympics instead of waiting another four years. Flo and six of her teammates didn't. They continued to practice and wait for the 1984 Olympics, which were scheduled to be in Los Angeles.

Flo kept improving. In 1981 she was named the world's best hitter. With her height and powerful right arm, she was almost unstoppable. Her five sisters and two brothers could hardly believe she was the same person who had been too shy and scared to try out for her high school team as a 14-year-old.

Finally 1984 arrived. Flo and the U.S. team went into the Games with high hopes. They had worked hard for a long time and they knew they were a good team.

The Chinese team was better. After a thrilling match, China won the gold medal.

Flo was proud of her silver medal, though, and she decided that now she could leave the U.S. national team. She went to Japan, where businesses paid players to play on their volleyball teams. Volleyball had always been her love, and Flo liked having it as her job too.

In Japan, while playing a volleyball game, Flo Hyman died. She was just 31 years old and very fit. But she had a heart disease she didn't even know about, called Marfan's syndrome. To remember Flo, the Women's Sports Foundation gives an award each year to a young female athlete.

Blocking

Blocking is a defensive move. Lisa is blocking, or trying to prevent a spiker from hitting the ball to her side of the court. Blockers also have to be careful not to touch the net.

Lisa watches the ball on the other side of the court and quickly moves to a spot opposite where the ball will be hit. She jumps straight up and spreads her fingers as wide as she can. A good block will prevent the ball from entering the blocking team's playing area, and it will fall back on the spiking team's side.

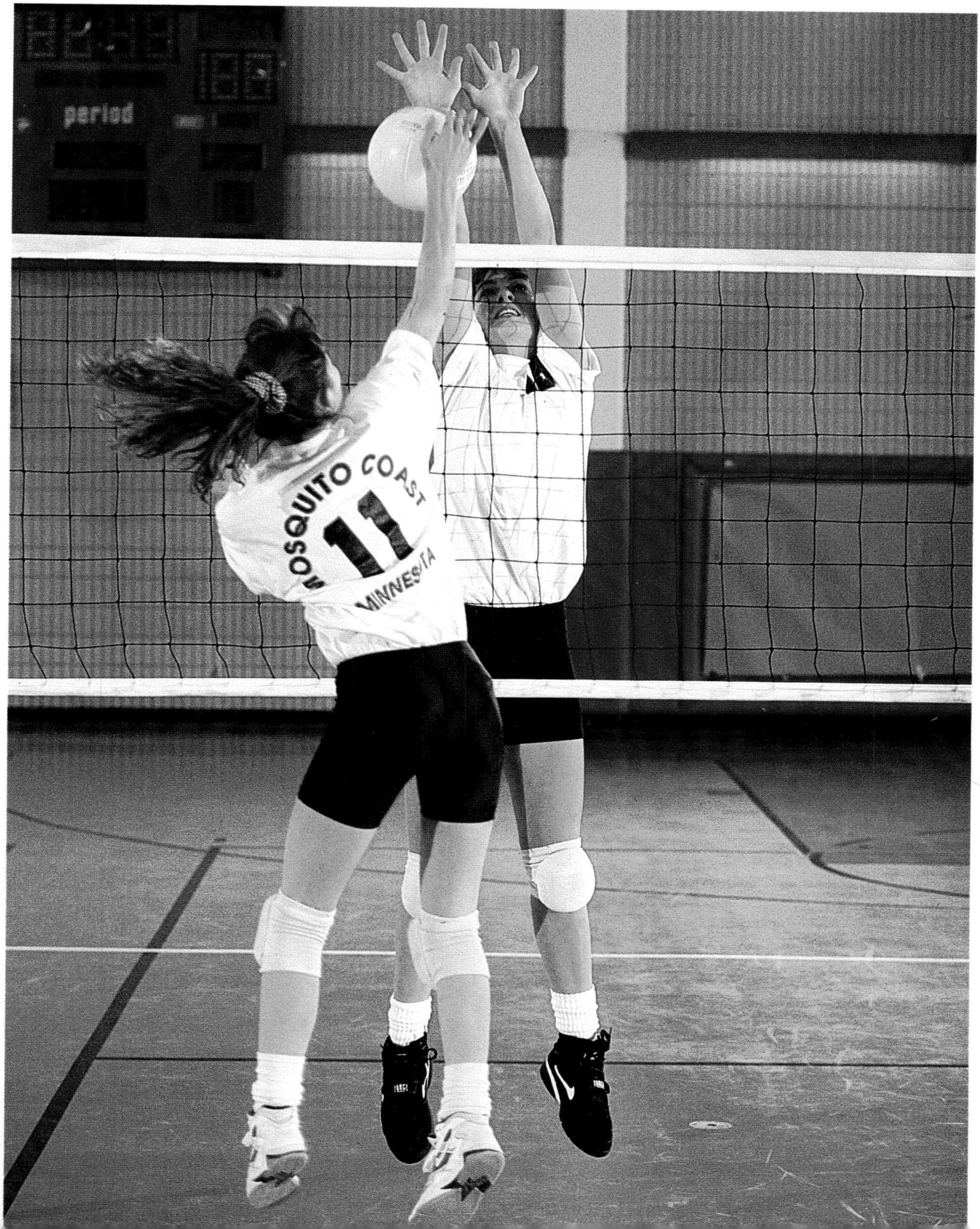
period
MOSQUITO COAST
11
MINNESOTA

Keep Your Eyes on the Ball

A good playing habit to develop is to always keep your eyes on the ball. Then you will be prepared to hit the ball if it comes in your direction. Try to keep watching the ball until after you have hit it.

Defense

The block is the first line of defense. If the ball does get past the blocker, the rest of the team must be ready for it. Good defensive players learn how to anticipate a shot. They figure out where the ball will land, and they move quickly to get under it.

Heather is a good defensive player. She bends her legs and stays low to the floor so she can dive for balls. Whenever possible, Heather uses both arms to pass the ball. She has learned that her passes are more likely to go where she wants them to if she uses two arms, as for a regular forearm pass, instead of sticking just one arm out.

But sometimes Heather has to really stretch to one side or the other to make a pass. That is called a **dig**. Heather gets only one arm or fist under the ball. She keeps that arm stiff and hits the ball with a fist or the heel of her hand. She tries to direct the ball high and toward the middle of her court, to where a team-mate can set it. Digs and other successful passes of difficult shots are called **saves**. For Heather and her teammates, saves are as exciting as spikes. They work hard on playing tough defense. The Mosqui-toes like to keep the play going, especi-ally when it seems almost impossible. Good defensive play wins games.

Chapter 3

GAME TIME

The Mosquito Coast team is getting ready to play in a tournament. At one of their practices, Coach McDonald splits the team into two teams for a practice game, or scrimmage. Coach McDonald will coach the Skeeters; Coach Shelley will coach the Coasters. Because it's a practice game, the two coaches also will call any violations.

The Skeeters win the coin toss, so they serve first. Barb's overhand serve is a good one. It goes over the net without touching it, and Barb quickly moves to the right back position.

The Coasters have trouble controlling Barb's serve. Instead of spiking it to the Skeeters' side of the court, the Coasters have to bump it over. Now the Skeeters are ready to try to score a point.

Coach McDonald has told the Skeeters that the best pattern of play is bump-set-spike. She wants the Skeeters to use all three of their hits, ending with a spike.

33

Janai uses an overhead pass to direct the ball to Sarah in the front row. Sarah sets the ball for Maura, who spikes the ball hard. It goes over the net and lands on the Coasters' court. The Skeeters are on the scoreboard!

Barb goes back behind the end line to serve. She will keep serving as long as her team is winning points. Barb delivers another good overhand serve, but this time the Coasters are ready for it. A Coaster back row player passes the ball to the setter. She gives one of the Coaster hitters a good set.

When the Coaster spiker jumps up to hit the ball, Charleen jumps up too. The ball slams into Charleen's hands and bounces back over the net, but it lands outside the sideline. Since Charleen last touched the ball before it landed out of bounds, the Coasters will now serve.

Winning the serve is called a sideout. After a **sideout**, the team about to serve must always rotate first. The players move clockwise one position and then the right back player serves.

Usually a back row player returns the serve, so Kristi, Janai, and Barb get ready. They watch the server, and are, in fact, on their toes.

The serve goes nearest to Janai, who runs to pass it. The ball was hit harder than she expected, however, and it bounces wildly off her arms and hits the ceiling. Coach McDonald blows her whistle. The Coasters have a point.

Janai shuffles her feet nervously. She thinks the Coaster server will serve the ball at her again. She's right.

Janai keeps her arms out in front of her and away from her body. The ball bounces cleanly off of Janai's arms this time. But because the ball was hit so hard, it bounces off Janai's arms and over the net. No bump-set-spike this time. Now the Skeeters must play defense.

Maura is blocking when the Coaster spiker jumps to hit the ball, but the other girl hits it to Maura's left. Kristi dives forward, her arms outstretched. The ball hits her arms and pops up. Sarah runs and bumps it to Maura, who swings and hits the ball. It ricochets off a Coasters' back row player and lands far off the court. Sideout for the Skeeters.

Maura steps behind the end line to serve. She's been working on her overhand serve and considers trying it now. But she decides her underhand serve is more reliable and uses it.

The Coasters return the ball with a crunching spike that gets between the Skeeters blockers and the net. The ball lands inbounds on the Skeeters' side of the net. Now the Coasters will serve.

This Coaster's serve seems to move from side to side as it comes toward the Skeeters. At first, Kristi thinks it's heading for her, but then it seems to move toward Jill. Kristi thinks Jill is going to pass the ball. Jill thinks Kristi is. The ball lands on the floor between them, and the Coasters have another point.

Coach McDonald signals for a time-out. After the Skeeters have huddled around her, she says, "Remember to call for the ball. Don't wait for a team-mate to take it. Call out 'Mine' and then pass it. Let's go."

On the next serve, Kristi yells "Mine" and passes the ball to the front row. Sarah sets the ball to Charleen, who hits it down on the Coaster side. Now the Skeeters are on the right track.

Passing Primer

Good passing leads to good play. To make sure you pass well, remember:

- *Watch the ball, and keep watching as it hits your arms.*
- *Try to anticipate where the ball will go and move quickly to beat it there.*
- *Bend your knees so you can keep your balance if the ball is hit hard.*
- *Face the direction you want the ball to go and aim it toward your target.*

Later in the game, the Skeeters are ahead 14–13. Maura is serving **game point,** which means that if the Skeeters win this point, they win the game.

Maura's serve, however, goes into the net. The Coasters score a point on their serve to tie the game at 14–14. Then the Skeeters get a sideout. Now Sarah will serve, but she won't be serving game point. The Skeeters now have to score two points to win.

Sarah's serve is a fast one. A Coaster back row player bumps the ball but it goes straight up in the air above her. A teammate rushes over and passes it to the front row, but all the spiker there can do is bump it over. The Skeeters are receiving a **free ball**—an easy ball to pass. Will they be able to set up a hard spike and score?

Sarah uses her overhead pass to relay the ball to Kristi. Janai wants to spike the ball and calls out "Yes, yes" to let Kristi know she's ready.

Kristi gently sends the ball out to Janai. It's a perfect set, five feet above the net and two feet from it. Janai jumps and swings her arm as rapidly as she can. Thwack. The ball lands on the Coasters' court for a Skeeter point.

Now Sarah is serving for game point. More than anything, she wants to make sure her serve is inbounds. She thinks about her last serve, which was a good one. She imagines tossing up the ball and hitting it solidly. She pretends that she sees the ball going over the net and landing on the Coasters' side.

When Coach McDonald blows her whistle to signal Sarah to serve, Sarah takes a deep breath. Then she tosses up the ball perfectly and hits it solidly. The ball goes over the net. But the Coasters are able to bump this serve and they set the ball up to one of their hitters.

When Janai sees that the hitter across from her will be spiking the ball, she bends her knees and prepares to block the ball. When the spiker is about to contact the ball, Janai springs up, fingers spread wide. The Coaster girl hits the ball into Janai's hands and it bounces back over the net and falls to the floor. The Skeeters win!

Chapter 4

PRACTICE, PRACTICE

Practices can't match games for excitement, but there are fun things players can do during practice to improve their volleyball skills. Some of these drills also help Heather, Danny, and their teammates to warm up before games.

Conditioning

Coach Stanek wants his players to be able to play long games without losing their energy. He knows that running builds endurance and stamina, so he tells his players to jog in place.

After running, the players are sweaty and warm. That's a good time for them to stretch their muscles. Stretching helps them become more flexible. Then, when they have to dive for a ball, their muscles can stretch without injury.

Coach Stanek also wants his players to be able to jump just as high at the end of a match as they can at the beginning. To do that, they have to strengthen their leg muscles. Jumping up and down does that. The players try to slap each other's hands above the net while being careful not to touch the net. Sometimes they jump rope.

Volleyball players also need strong hands and fingers. To strengthen his finger muscles, Danny makes tight fists and then opens his fingers wide. He also squeezes rubber balls, such as tennis balls, to build up those muscles.

Drills

The Team 'Sota players are practicing their serves. They have put a chair on each side of the court. Players serve from both ends of the court. They try to hit the chair opposite them with their serve.

Passing is another skill that Team 'Sota works on often. The drill the players like the most keeps them moving.

Some players line up, one behind the other. Other players line up facing them. The two lines are about 10 feet apart. David tosses the ball to Bob, then runs and stands at the end of Bob's line. Bob passes the ball to Kris. Then Bob goes to the end of Kris's line. The routine continues in a figure eight until the ball hits the floor. The players work on controlling their passes so that they can keep the ball moving. As they get better, they move farther apart. Sometimes they do this drill using overhead passes. This drill helps them develop controlled, accurate passing skills.

The Mosquito Coast players practice passing with a passing line. Sarah is ready to pass. Coach McDonald hits the ball over the net from the other side. Sarah passes the ball to a teammate standing at the net. When Sarah has made five good passes, she goes to the net to catch the balls and her teammate practices passing.

Coach Stanek has Team 'Sota do that drill too, but he adds setting and hitting practice. Coach Stanek hits the ball across the net to the passer. The passer passes the ball to the setter, who sets the ball for the hitter. After the hitter has hit the ball, the players rotate. The passer becomes the setter, and the setter becomes the hitter. The hitter goes to the passer's position.

All the Mosquitoes love to practice spiking. One of the Mosquitoes stands near the net to set the ball. The other girls stand in a line.

Janai is first in line at the attack line. She tosses the ball to Sarah so that it is right above her head. Sarah sets the ball for Janai, who spikes it over. Then it's Heather's turn. The Mosquitoes also take turns practicing their blocking while the others are hitting.

Charleen and the other Mosquitoes also love to play "pepper" with a friend. Charleen, Lisa, and Deanna are playing pepper to warm up before a game. They are standing about five feet away from each other. Charleen tosses the ball to Lisa and she bumps or sets the ball to Deanna, who bumps or sets the ball back to Charleen. They practice passing, setting, and hitting it at each other. Nobody wants to be the one to let the ball hit the floor, so they also get to practice their spectacular dives and saves.

If a partner isn't available, Charleen plays pepper against the wall. When she spikes the ball at the wall, however, she has to hit it so that the ball bounces on the floor first. Then the ball will bounce off the wall and return to her. Since the wall never misses, Charleen prefers to play with Lisa.

Team 'Sota often ends its practices with a fast-paced game that wears out everyone. The players get into teams of three. Coach Stanek hits the ball to one of the teams, and then the two teams play out a point. The team that loses the point has to leave the court. Another team quickly replaces it, and Coach Stanek starts another point.

Chapter 5

RAZZLE DAZZLE

Danny, Sarah, and their teammates sometimes go to high school or college matches. There they see some advanced moves that make the games even more exciting. The players work on these advanced skills in practice.

Jump Serve

Becky's favorite move is the **jump serve**. She's working on it in practice and Coach McDonald says she'll master it if she keeps trying. The jump serve takes lots of practice.

Jump Serving Star

Karch Kiraly was one of the first American players to make the jump serve popular. Karch joined the U.S. men's national team in 1981. He and teammate Steve Timmons led the U.S. men to two Olympic gold medals. He was named the Most Valuable Player in the 1988 Olympics, when the United States defeated the former Soviet Union for the gold.

Karch is a versatile player who passes and spikes very well. But what many of his fans like best is his jump serve. He adds his own special flair by tossing the ball up with one hand while the other is on his hip.

Karch left the U.S. team after the 1988 Olympics to play for an Italian professional team. He returned to the United States with his wife, Janna, and their two sons. Now, he plays beach volleyball for a living.

Coach McDonald tells Becky to begin the jump serve holding the ball in both hands. Then, Becky throws the ball up, about five feet above her head and about a foot in front of her. Now, Becky pretends she's spiking. She jumps and hits the ball, just like in a spike, except now Becky can jump forward. She doesn't have to worry about hitting the net.

Tips

Deanna likes the ferocious spikes the best. She has noticed that sometimes when a spiker jumps up for a spike, instead of slamming the ball down she will lightly tap it over the net with her fingertips. Because the blocker and the other defenders are expecting a hard hit, they aren't ready for the soft shot. These shots are called **tips,** or **dinks**.

Coach McDonald tells Deanna to keep her wrist and elbow locked when she practices this move. Just her fingertips flick the ball over.

Back Sets

Back sets are what Danny likes to watch for in the high school and college matches. He works on back sets at every practice. A back set starts out just like a regular set. But when Danny contacts the ball, he pushes it over his head and back instead of in front of him. At the same time, he pushes his hips forward and arches his back. His follow-through is up and back. That sends the ball to the hitter behind the setter.

Some of the setters really fool their opponents so that the blockers jump up in the wrong spots. Sometimes even Danny can't tell when a back set is coming. That's because experienced setters can disguise them.

55

Chapter 6

MORE WAYS TO PLAY

Six is the usual number of players on a side, but there are other types of volleyball teams. Some people use four players on a team. They are positioned in a diamond pattern with one player at the net, two side players halfway down the sidelines, and a back player in the middle of the end line. The players rotate to serve, and only the front three players can spike and block.

Players also play with three to a side. This is called triples. In this type of game, the player in the middle stays by the net to block and set. The other two players pass the ball and spike. The players still must rotate before they serve.

Another variation is doubles, in which there are two players on each side. Players take turns serving. Both players pass, set, and spike.

Barbra Fontana (facing page) and Karch Kiraly (above) compete on the pro beach volleyball tour.

Volleyball also can be played outside a gym. In California and Florida, many people play volleyball on the beach. It takes a little practice to play on the sand in bare feet.

Beach volleyball is so popular that some men and women are paid to play. The professional beach volleyball players play in tournaments for prize money. There are both men's and women's pro leagues.

People also play volleyball on grass, in backyards or parks. There are lots of places to play volleyball. One good way to get started is to talk to the physical education teacher at your school. He or she can suggest places for you to play.

Often recreation centers or community playgrounds have volleyball leagues. Stop in at a rec center close to your home and ask about opportunities to get started in volleyball.

There is also a nationwide program for young players that is run by the United States Volleyball Association. Look in the telephone book for the number of the USVBA in your area.

Junior high schools and high schools often have volleyball teams that play other schools. Some high school players continue to play volleyball in college. Sometimes they receive scholarships to play on volleyball teams.

A few players who are very talented and dedicated end up playing on the Olympic team or in professional leagues. You could be one of them.

Or you may find yourself in a rec center gym, playing for fun and fitness. Either way, knowing the right moves makes volleyball a terrific sport for a lifetime.

VOLLEYBALL TALK

approach: A series of quick, running steps a hitter takes before spiking the ball.

attack line: A line about 3 meters, or 10 feet, from the net.

back set: A set that goes behind the setter's head.

block: To try to prevent the other team's spike from coming across the net by jumping up and letting the ball hit your hands.

center line: The line on the court directly beneath the net.

dig: A return or pass of a hard-hit ball.

dink: A gentle hit after jumping as if to spike it; also called a **tip**.

fault: An illegal move or play.

first referee: The official in charge of the match; stands on a ladder or small platform at one end of the net.

follow through: To continue a motion after contacting the ball.

forearm pass: A hit with straight forearms in front of your body; also called a bump pass.

free ball: A returned ball that is easy to play.

game point: The point that will win the game.

jump serve: A serve in which the server tosses the ball and then jumps to hit it.

line judge: The official who watches to see where the ball lands. Usually, there are two line judges for a game.

match: A series of games played between two teams. The first team to win two games in a three-game match or three games in a five-game match wins the match.

overhand serve: A serve in which the server tosses the ball and hits it when it is above his or her head but doesn't jump to hit it.

overhead pass: A pass made by contacting the ball with only the fingertips and directing it to a teammate.

pass: To hit the ball to a teammate, either with an overhead pass or a forearm pass.

rotate: To move one position clockwise.

save: To keep the ball from hitting the floor, usually with a dive or dig.

scorekeeper: The official who keeps track of how many points each team has during a game.

second referee: The official who stands on the floor at one end of the net.

serve: To put the ball in play by hitting it directly over the net and into the other team's court.

set: To put the ball in position for a teammate to hit it over the net.

sideout: Winning the chance to serve.

spike: To forcefully hit the ball over the net.

10-foot line: Line about 3 meters, or 10 feet, from the net; also called **attack line**.

tip: To gently hit the ball over the net after jumping as if to spike it; also called a **dink**.

underhand serve: A serve in which the server tosses the ball and hits it by swinging his or her arm forward below the waist.

FURTHER READING

Bertucci, Bob. *Championship Volley-ball: By the Experts*. West Point, New York: Leisure Press, 1982.

Egstrom, Glen H., and Frances Schaafsma. *Volleyball*. Wm. C. Brown Publishers, 1984.

Kiraly, Karch. *Karch Kiraly's Championship Volleyball*. New York: Simon & Schuster Inc., 1990.

Lucas, Jeff. *Pass, Set, Crush: Volleyball Illustrated*. Euclid Northwest Publications, 1988.

Lyttle, Richard. *Basic Volleyball Strategy*. Garden City, New York: Doubleday, 1979.

Scates, Allen E. *Winning Volleyball*. Newton, Massachusetts: Allyn and Bacon, Inc., 1984.

FOR MORE INFORMATION

United States Volleyball Association
3595 East Fountain Boulevard
Colorado Springs, CO 80910

INDEX